A Note From Rick Renner

I am on a personal quest to see a "revival of the Bible" so people can establish their lives on a firm foundation that will stand strong and endure the test as end-time storm winds begin to intensify.

In order to experience a revival of the Bible in your personal life, it is important to take time each day to read, receive, and apply its truths to your life. James tells us that if we will continue in the perfect law of liberty — refusing to be forgetful hearers, but determined to be doers — we will be blessed in our ways. As you watch or listen to the programs in this series and work through this corresponding study guide, I trust you will search the Scriptures and allow the Holy Spirit to help you hear something new from God's Word that applies specifically to your life. I encourage you to be a doer of the Word He reveals to you. Whatever the cost, I assure you — it will be worth it.

> Thy words were found, and I did eat them;
> and thy word was unto me the joy and rejoicing of mine heart:
> for I am called by thy name, O Lord God of hosts.
> — Jeremiah 15:16

Your brother and friend in Jesus Christ,

Rick Renner

Unless otherwise indicated, all scripture quotations are taken from the *King James Version* of the Bible.

Scripture quotations marked (*AMPC*) are taken from the *Amplified*® Bible. Copyright © 1954, 1958, 1962, 1964, 1965, 1987 by The Lockman Foundation. Used by permission. www.Lockman.org.

Scripture quotations marked (*NIV*) are taken from the *Holy Bible, New International Version*®, *NIV*® Copyright ©1973, 1978, 1984, 2011 by Biblica, Inc.® Used by permission. All rights reserved worldwide.

Scripture quotations marked *RIV* are taken from *Renner Interpretive Version*. Copyright © 2021 by Rick Renner.

What You Need in Your Spiritual Diet

Copyright © 2023 by Rick Renner
1814 W. Tacoma St.
Broken Arrow, OK 74012-1406

Published by Rick Renner Ministries
www.renner.org

ISBN 13: 978-1-6675-0321-9

eBook ISBN 13: 978-1-6675-0322-6

Printed in the United States of America. All rights reserved. No portion of this book may be reproduced or transmitted in any form or by any means — electronic, mechanical, photocopy, recording, scanning, or other — except for brief quotations in critical reviews or articles, without the prior written permission of the Publisher.

How To Use This Study Guide

This five-lesson study guide corresponds to *"What You Need in Your Spiritual Diet" With Rick Renner* (Renner TV). Each lesson in this study guide covers a topic that is addressed during the program series, with questions and references supplied to draw you deeper into your own private study of the Scriptures on this subject.

To derive the most benefit from this study guide, consider the following:

First, watch or listen to the program prior to working through the corresponding lesson in this guide. (Programs can also be viewed at **renner.org** by clicking on the Media/Archive links or on our Renner Ministries YouTube Channel.)

Second, take the time to look up the scriptures included in each lesson. Prayerfully consider their application to your own life.

Third, use a journal or notebook to make note of your answers to each lesson's Study Questions and Practical Application challenges.

Fourth, invest specific time in prayer and in the Word of God to consult with the Holy Spirit. Write down the scriptures or insights He reveals to you.

Finally, take action! Whatever the Lord tells you to do according to His Word, do it.

For added insights on this subject, it is recommended that you obtain Rick Renner's book *Unlikely — Our Faith-Filled Journey to the Ends of the Earth*. You may also select from Rick's other available resources by placing your order at **renner.org** or by calling 1-800-742-5593.

LESSON 1

TOPIC

Spend Time With God Every Day

SCRIPTURES
1. **Psalm 5:3** — My voice shalt thou hear in the morning, O Lord; in the morning will I direct my prayer unto thee, and will look up.
2. **Psalm 3:3** — But thou, O Lord, art a shield for me; my glory, and the lifter up of mine head.
3. **1 Corinthians 6:19** — …Your body is the temple of the Holy Ghost which is in you, which ye have of God, and ye are not your own?

GREEK WORDS
No Greek words were shown on the TV program.

SYNOPSIS
Taking care of our physical body is important; we need to exercise and maintain a good diet to stay healthy. We need to take care of our spirit in the same way. To ensure that our spiritual diet is healthy, we need to *spend time with God every day, be quiet and pray, do things for others, say "no" to things*, and *stir up the gift of God inside us*. When we practice these things in our daily lives, we allow for God to work — not just in our spiritual life, but in ways we can see in our physical life as well!

The emphasis of this lesson is:

Just as developing healthy eating habits is important for maintaining physical strength, likewise, there are things that you need to develop in your spiritual diet that will make you both stronger and healthier. In this lesson, you will learn about the first spiritual ingredient — spending time with God every day. In fact, this is the most important ingredient in cultivating a healthy and strong spiritual diet. And it's best that you spend time with God in the mornings.

Start Your Day Looking Up

We're living in some challenging times, and some might consider these to be some of the most challenging times that any believer has ever faced. In a very difficult season in Rick's life, he learned to develop certain disciplines to give him spiritual strength. One of these disciplines was to learn to spend time with God every single day — not just every day, but *in the mornings*. He learned that if he would incorporate this into his life, he would become strong in the Lord. However, it is important to note that the only way you can master such a discipline is if you make a commitment to do so.

Here's the amazing thing, God is *always* blessed when you bring Him the first fruits of anything. And when you give God the first fruits of your day, He sees to it that the rest of your day is multiplied so that you may accomplish what you wouldn't normally be able to accomplish. But what does it mean to spend time with God every single day? The Bible gives a great example of this in Psalm 5:3.

In Psalm 5:3, David said, "My voice shalt thou hear in the morning, O Lord; in the morning will I direct my prayer unto thee, and will look up." Notice the last statement where David said, "…And will look up." David knew that the first thing he needed to do each morning was to look up to the Lord, and *so do you!*

David was surrounded by enemies both inside and outside of his house; he had struggles with the men on his staff, in his marriage, in his relationships, with his children, and with enemy forces who longed to see him destroyed. And we know from reading the Book of Psalms that David was also tempted to struggle emotionally. He learned that if he didn't begin the day by looking up to the Lord, he would often very quickly become frustrated and begin looking down. It's a simple fact of life that things have a way of speeding out of control very, very quickly when we become discouraged and down. That is why it's so very important that before you even lift your head off the pillow or put your feet on the floor — *you must make a commitment to look up.* You have to make a concrete decision that this is the first thing you're going to do every single morning.

God Is the Lifter of Your Head

In Psalm 3:3, David said, "But thou, O Lord, art a shield for me; my glory, and the lifter of mine head." This verse tells us that God is the lifter of our head. And if you'll make a commitment to look up first thing every morning, He will help you keep your head held high the whole day through!

You might say, "Well, I'm just not a morning person." Even so, you can become a morning person — *and it will change your life!* To do this you may have to go to bed a little bit earlier or turn the television off at night so you can get up earlier. But ask yourself, what value does watching television until midnight add to your life — if any at all? Television is a major time consumer. It fills your brain with information you don't really need and your eyes with things that aren't going to make any difference in your life, and watching too much television can cause you to go to bed late, which in turn causes you to wake up late. So why not turn the TV off earlier, put your phone down, and go to bed?

Instead of watching TV, talk to the Lord before you go to sleep and wake up early so that you can spend a little time with Him in the morning as well. And spending time with the Lord doesn't mean you need to spend hours there. Begin with two minutes or begin with five minutes, but before you do anything else — *consecrate the first part of your day to look up.*

Rick's Morning Routine

The following text contains some of Rick Renner's best practices for spending quality, personal time with God in the mornings.

When Rick wakes up in the morning, before he ever lifts his head off the pillow, he acknowledges the presence of the Lord in his life. He says, "Lord, thank you for your presence. I thank you that you are the Lord of this day." Recognizing that Jesus is Lord of the day and whatever happens in the day is a great way to begin the morning!

Rick then prays for Denise, for their sons, for their sons' wives, for his and Denise's grandchildren, and for his siblings and their families. He also prays for the partners of the ministry, for you, and for everyone who watches the TV program. Rick has a whole list of people he prays for each and every day — *all before he ever lifts his head off the pillow or places his feet on the ground.*

Now, you may be thinking, *Wow, that must take a long time!* But it doesn't take long at all! It only takes Rick about a minute or two to go through each of these things as he prays. It comes from his heart, and it comes very quickly — *but it's prayed with faith, it's very sincere, and it really means something.* When you start your day in prayer, it lays down a different foundation for your day — it changes your attitude for what's ahead of you because you know that you started your day right.

After Rick prays for his family, he goes into the kitchen to turn on the coffee pot. It takes about two or three minutes for the coffee to brew, so during that time, he does push-ups. This is because the Bible says that your body is the temple of the Holy Ghost who lives inside you and you are not your own (*see* 1 Corinthians 6:19). The truth is, your body is the temple of the Holy Ghost, and if you want your temple to be in good shape, *you must do something to keep it that way.* Rick made a decision years ago that he would begin every day by exercising. Again, this doesn't take up a lot of time, and it's amazing how much of a difference it makes in your prayer life, your spiritual life, and your physical life!

Once his coffee is ready, Rick grabs the pot and his coffee cup and walks into his room where he takes his Bible and immediately begins to read the Scriptures. Rick built this discipline by self-imposing this rule in his life: no Bible, no breakfast. This is not a rule written in Scripture anywhere, but it's a rule that has helped Rick form this habit in his life. If Rick doesn't read his Bible, no food goes into his mouth. This is just an example of a discipline that Rick personally knew he needed and incorporated into his morning routine, and maybe you need it too.

Self-imposing a rule such as "no Bible, no breakfast" will help you pick up your Bible and read it. And if you don't know where to start reading, ask your church for a Bible reading plan or contact RENNER Ministries and we'll provide one for you. Having a plan will help you stay on track and act as a type of personal accountability. And there are so many benefits to reading the Word of God. Reading it every day will feed you, help you stay on track, and keep your heart soft before the Lord.

Praying, exercising, and reading the Bible each day are requirements for Rick's RENNER Ministries leadership team. Every day, Rick asks his team members, "Did you read your Bible? Did you pray in tongues? Did you exercise?" And his team asks him the same questions. Every morning they hold each other accountable to at least these three things, as they are essential to every believer's spiritual diet.

Spending Time With God Is Essential for Everyone

Spending time with God is *not* an option. Often those in ministry make the mistake of thinking that the time they take to prepare to preach to others is their personal devotion time — it is not. You need *personal* time with the Lord for your own heart, not just time spent preparing to serve someone else. Many good people in ministry have fallen into the trap of thinking that if they spend time in preparation, that is the equivalent of feeding themselves. But the truth is, you need time to pray and to feed on the Word of God and to fellowship with the Lord — *just for you*.

Many people might not know where to start, saying, "Well, if I need to read the Bible every day, what should I read?" The following are suggestions for whatever situation you may be going through: If you need wisdom, then read the book of Proverbs — Proverbs is full of wisdom. If you need strength, read the Book of Psalms because the Book of Psalms is filled with strength. If you want a deeper revelation of Jesus, His life, and His ministry, then read the four gospels. Reading the Scriptures will take you deep into God's presence as you spend time with Him.

Before you start reading, pray and ask the Holy Spirit to open your eyes as you read and pray. And after you finish reading, say, "Holy Spirit, show me how to incorporate what I've read into my personal life." Remember not to rush your time with the Lord — *take your time and really read*. Meditate on what you're reading, and if you can memorize it, then begin to speak it out of your mouth. Also, if you're using a Bible reading plan and come to a particular chapter that you feel is a little challenging or difficult to understand, read that chapter in a different translation. A different translation may be able to impart what you've read to you in a new, fresher way. And if you feel like you need to pause on a verse a little bit longer, that's alright! Pause and get that verse into your heart until you get everything you could possibly need out of it.

You need to let the Word of God fill your eyes, fill your mind, and touch your emotions — *you need to let the Word of God change you.* That's why Rick ends every program quoting Ecclesiastes 8:4, "Where the word of a king is, there is power...." *God's Word has the power to transform you.*

The most important ingredient you need in your spiritual diet is time with God. You may not know exactly how to do that, and that's why this lesson's focus is to teach you practical instructions about how you can spend time with God. Spending time with the Lord each morning is simple, and it will totally revolutionize and transform your life. So after completing this lesson, be encouraged to make a commitment to prioritize your time with Him and lay hold of this vital ingredient in your spiritual diet.

STUDY QUESTIONS

> Study to shew thyself approved unto God, a workman that needeth not to be ashamed, rightly dividing the word of truth.
> — 2 Timothy 2:15

1. What is the number one thing you need to do every day in order to stay strong spiritually?
2. Why is spending time with God in the morning so important, as opposed to spending time with Him other times of the day?
3. What does it look like to spend time with God daily? What are some examples Rick gave from his morning routine?

PRACTICAL APPLICATION

> But be ye doers of the word, and not hearers only, deceiving your own selves.
> — James 1:22

1. What are some things you can change in your daily routine to make setting apart time in the morning to commune with God easier? List them here.
2. Rick teaches that he made a self-imposed rule for himself to encourage him to read his Bible every day. What are some possible self-imposed rules that you can make in your life to encourage yourself to read the Bible each day? List them below.

LESSON 2

TOPIC
Be Quiet and Pray

SCRIPTURES
1. **1 Thessalonians 5:17** — Pray without ceasing.
2. **Philippians 4:6 (*NLT*)** — Don't worry about anything; instead, pray about everything. Tell God what you need, and thank him for all he has done.
3. **Ephesians 6:18 (*AMPC*)** — Pray at all times (on every occasion, in every season)....
4. **Proverbs 27:19** — As in water face answereth to face, so the heart of man to man.
5. **Psalm 46:10** — Be still, and know that I am God....
6. **Psalm 37:4** — Delight thyself also in the Lord: and he shall give thee the desires of thine heart.

GREEK WORDS
No Greek words were shown on the TV program.

SYNOPSIS
In this lesson, we're going to look at the next ingredient that you need in your spiritual life — *to be quiet and pray*. You might think, *Is being quiet really that important?* In fact, it is very, very important. In the previous lesson, we learned about the importance of spending time with the Lord in the morning, and in today's lesson, we'll be diving deeper into the importance of prayer. This ingredient is crucial to have in your life. Prayer shouldn't just be a daily activity that you check off your to-do list. You need to have a lifestyle of prayer because, as we'll see in this lesson, *prayer is meant to be a way of life.*

The emphasis of this lesson is:

There are certain things you need in your spiritual diet. Number one: you must spend time with the Lord. Number two: you must be quiet

and pray. The ingredient of prayer is vital to your spiritual life. Leading a lifestyle of prayer and carving out quiet moments to spend with God will allow Him to work in your life.

What Does It Mean To 'Pray Without Ceasing'?

First Thessalonians 5:17 says, "Pray without ceasing." You may be wondering, *How do you pray without ceasing?* Literally, the words "without ceasing" mean *continuously, without interruption,* or *without taking a break.* But this doesn't mean you have to go through the entire day with your eyes closed praying. You can actually pray while you're doing many different things.

You can pray before you read your Bible. Praying before reading your Bible is a great opportunity to ask the Holy Spirit to open your eyes so that you may behold wonderous things (*see* Psalm 119:18). If you involve the Holy Spirit in your daily Bible reading, He will empower you to see things you wouldn't normally see by yourself.

You can also pray as you read your Bible, asking, "Holy Spirit, what does that mean?" or saying, "Holy Spirit, please help me to understand that." You can pray with your spouse. Rick shared in the program that he doesn't go to bed without speaking the name of Jesus over Denise. And when he wakes up and finishes his personal prayer, again, Rick will pray over Denise, saying, "I ask you to bless Denise and to be with us and help us be productive today." Rick prays with Denise every day, and if you have a spouse, you should make it a priority to pray with them every day too.

You can pray with your children. If you have children at home, pray with them before they leave the house. When Rick's boys were young, they never walked out the front door without Rick and Denise taking them by the hand and quoting parts of Psalm 91 to them. They would pray, "With long life will God satisfy you and show you His salvation. He will give His angels charge over you and keep you in all of your ways" (*see* Psalm 91:11,16).

You can also pray before you get in your car. Those who know Rick know that he doesn't pull out of the driveway without first pleading the blood of Jesus over his car and praying for the drivers around him as well as for himself. You can even pray before you board a plane! Whenever Rick boards a plane, he touches the aircraft, speaking the name of Jesus over it and the crew. *This* is what it means to pray without ceasing — it is a state of being in constant communication with the Lord. And this is why Paul instructed early believers to pray without ceasing (*see* 1 Thessalonians 5:17).

Again, prayer is meant to be our way of life, and the Bible confirms this. Philippians 4:6 (*NLT*) tells us, "Don't worry about anything; instead, pray about everything. Tell God what you need, and thank him for all he has done." Ephesians 6:18 (*AMPC*) says, "Pray at all times (on every occasion, in every season)...." The *Renner Interpretive Version* (*RIV*) even says to pray every chance you get. To reiterate, you can pray for your spouse, your marriage, your children, your grandchildren, your leaders, your pastor, your local officials, your governor, your president, and your unsaved family members and friends to come to Christ (just to name a few). You can even pray for financial provision — and if you're praying about it, *why worry about it?*

You can pray for understanding and revelation of the Word of God, or you can pray for angelic protection. No matter the topic — *pray, pray, pray.* Pray as you're on the move — pray as a way of life — and don't wait for a crisis to arise to begin praying. You can pray about anything at any time because anything that concerns you concerns the Lord. Whatever is on your mind, just talk to Him about it!

The Power of Being Quiet

In your spiritual life, you also need the daily ingredient of being quiet. You might be wondering, *What does that mean?* The Bible gives us a helpful example of this in Proverbs 27:19, "As in water face answereth to face, so the heart of man to man." If you look down into a pool that has a lot of movement or activity, there are a lot of ripples and you have a distorted image. But when the water becomes really, really still, you can look into the water and see a clear image of yourself. Likewise, when your life is filled with a lot of ripples, sometimes you can't see things clearly, and that's why you need to let things get still, or quiet, so you can see clearly.

Ask yourself, "Do I ever take time to be quiet?" If not, you need to — even if it's only for a few minutes each day. One reason that people get confused or stressed is because they're never quiet. They get so busy that they're no longer in touch with who they are, what they're feeling, what they need, or what they believe. They become like robots going through the motions of life.

We all need to slow down, not just to be in touch with the Lord, but to be in touch with ourselves. The truth is, deep contemplation is needed by *all of us* in order to stay in touch with our own hearts. And when we're still, all the ripples in our life begin to go away, and we're able to see what's really going on inside of us. Sometimes we get confused because we don't understand what's going on inside of us. But when we're quiet, God has the opportunity to reveal to us what we need to know. Too much activity without any pause leads to spiritual dullness and confusion. That's why being quiet is such a valuable and important ingredient in maintaining a thriving spiritual life!

Get Creative With How To Be Quiet

You may be wondering, *When am I going to find time to be quiet?* To begin, you might have to carve it out of your schedule, but you can do it — *you can even start with just a minute or two*!

Maybe you're also thinking, *Okay, one or two minutes is doable, but where can I find a moment of quietness?* Do you have a bathroom? Go in the bathroom and lock the door. Let it be the place where you're going to be quiet. And if people knock on the door, then truthfully tell them that you're taking care of business. You don't need to tell them what kind of business, just let them know you're busy and take that as your moment to be quiet. Or, during your lunch break, take a walk where you can clear your mind and be quiet even if you have to go in a closet and shut the door.

Rick shared that sometimes when he can't find Denise she is on the floor in the closet trying to get a few moments of quiet time with the Lord. Maybe you can do the same, or maybe you can sit in the car by yourself and steal a moment of quietness. You could even choose to get up before everyone else in your house and sit quietly by yourself. That's what Rick does every day.

Sometimes you have to get creative to find a moment of quietness, but it can be done. And remember, every person in your home needs a moment of stillness, so be sure to grant them what they need to be quiet and to be by themselves too.

Being Still Creates Space for Revelation

Psalm 46:10 reads, "Be still, and know that I am God…." According to this verse, there are some things about God you're only going to discover by being still. *Are you still enough for God to reveal things about Himself to you?* If not, begin setting aside time in your day — even if it's only two minutes a day — to be alone with the Lord and to be alone with yourself.

In Psalm 37:4, David said, "Delight thyself also in the Lord: and he shall give thee the desires of thine heart." God will give you the desires of your heart, but to receive them you must first know what those desires are! If you never slow down long enough to be quiet, you will probably be confused about the desires of your heart. And when you're unsure about these desires, your prayers may seem confusing or indecisive too. One day you might say you want one thing, and the next day you say you want something else — you go back and forth because you've not been still long enough to get a revelation of the true desires of your heart.

There are so many things you're only going to find out about yourself and your own desires by slowing down long enough to be quiet so that your heart can begin to speak to you. And your heart will speak to you if you'll get quiet. If you're not in touch with your own heart, how can you know what your desires are or what you should be believing for? This is why it is so important to carve out moments of being quiet in your life. Being quiet and developing prayer as a lifestyle are vital ingredients in your spiritual diet. It may not seem like a great feat to carve out a moment of quietness, but it is! And once you do, it will totally revolutionize your life.

STUDY QUESTIONS

Study to shew thyself approved unto God, a workman that needeth not to be ashamed, rightly dividing the word of truth.
— 2 Timothy 2:15

1. What does it mean to "pray without ceasing"?
2. Why is it so important to make time for prayer every single day? How does this contribute to having a strong spiritual diet?
3. Why is being quiet, or still, important? What does being quiet allow you to do?

PRACTICAL APPLICATION

But be ye doers of the word, and not hearers only, deceiving your own selves.
— James 1:22

1. In this lesson, Rick gives several examples of how to live a lifestyle of prayer. List some ways you can incorporate prayer into your daily life.
2. You learned the importance of being quiet in this lesson. While it may seem hard to fit quiet time into your daily schedule, you can start by carving out just a few minutes of quiet. What are some opportunities you can take in your day to be quiet and pray? List them and put them into practice today.

LESSON 3

TOPIC

Do Something for Someone Else

SCRIPTURES

1. **Philippians 2:4** — Look not every man on his own things, but every man also on the things of others.
2. **Philippians 2:19** — But I trust in the Lord Jesus to send Timotheus shortly unto you, that I also may be of good comfort, when I know your state.
3. **Philippians 2:20** — For I have no man likeminded, who will naturally care for your state.
4. **Philippians 2:21** — For all seek their own….
5. **1 Peter 4:9** — Use hospitality one to another without grudging.
6. **1 Peter 4:9 (*RIV*)** — Be reciprocally helpful and hospitable especially to fellow believers who find themselves in foreign or unfamiliar territory, who are out of their natural element, or who are in a struggling position, and do it without the accompaniment of begrudging, bellyaching, groaning, grumbling, moaning, or griping under your breath.
7. **1 Peter 4:10** — As every man hath received the gift, even so minister the same one to another, as good stewards of the manifold grace of God.
8. **1 Peter 4:10 (*RIV*)** — Accordingly, as every single one of you (with no exceptions) has received a grace-given charisma, you need to continuously minister to and serve one another with those gifts to the best of your ability and with the highest possible standard. God has assigned this great responsibility to you, so administrate and manage what He

has entrusted to you as outstanding managers of the assorted, diverse, various, variegated, multifaceted, and multicolored manifestations of the grace of God.

GREEK WORDS

1. "use hospitality" — φιλόξενος (*philoxenos*): a compound of φίλος (*philos*) and ξένος (*xenos*); the word φίλος (*philos*) is the word for a friend or to be friendly, and the word ξένος (*xenos*) depicts an alien either living in or passing through a foreign city or country, thus, a foreigner, or it could also be translated as guest, stranger, or traveler; as a compound, it depicts the attitude and actions of one who is helpful and hospitable to aliens in a foreign city or country, one who is helpful and hospitable to those who are out of their element, one who is helpful and hospitable to strangers, or even one who is helpful and hospitable to anyone in a struggling position

2. "one to another" — ἀλλήλους (*allelous*): one to another; it describes a reciprocal behavior that is to be mutually exchanged between believers when a need arises

3. "without" — ἄνευ (*aneu*): a preposition that means to do something in accompaniment, cooperation, or in parallel to another action; here, Peter commands all believers not to sing a bad duet of helping others with a resentful attitude

4. "grudging" — γογγυσμός (*gongusmos*): to begrudge, complain, grumble, loathe, moan, and groan, or to quietly mutter resentment under one's breath; in context, it pictures one who accommodates those who are struggling, but rather than do it joyfully, he does it with the accompaniment of silent resentment, inward complaining, grumbling, and muttering under his breath

5. "every man" — ἕκαστος (*hekastos*): an all-inclusive term that embraces everyone with no one excluded

6. "gift" — χάρισμα (*charisma*): derived from the word χάρις (*charis*), the Greek word for grace, but as χάρισμα (*charisma*), it speaks of grace-given gifts

7. "minister" — διακονέω (*diakoneo*): a servant whose primary responsibility is to serve food and wait on tables; presents a picture of a waiter who painstakingly attends to the needs and wishes of the patron; it was such a servant's supreme task to please clients, therefore, he served honorably, pleasurably, and in a fashion that made the people

he waited on feel as if they were nobility; this is a committed, professional server who is zealously dedicated to doing his job on the highest level possible

8. "manifold" — ποικίλος (*poikilos*): assorted, diverse, various, variegated, or multicolored; a form of it is used in the Old Testament Greek Septugint to describe Joseph's coat of many colors; Peter used it here to denote the assorted, diverse, various, variegated, multifaceted, or multicolored gifts of grace that God has entrusted to His people

SYNOPSIS

In this lesson, we're going to focus on the third essential ingredient that you need in your spiritual life — *doing something for someone else*. It may seem at first like a trivial ingredient, but you will learn that God has gifted you and you need to be using your gifts not only for yourself but also to bless others around you. It is not simply a suggestion — it is a command for every believer to be helpful and hospitable to those in need, those who are in an unfamiliar place, and those who are in a struggling position.

The emphasis of this lesson is:

The next crucial ingredient you need in your spiritual diet is to do something for someone else. This ingredient is important because it causes you to make an effort to keep your mind off of yourself and, instead, focus on the needs of others around you. We are called by God and His Word to use our God-given gifts to serve those around us, especially those who may be struggling or who are in a difficult season of their lives. And it is essential that while serving others, you have a humble attitude — that your service is not accompanied by complaining and groaning.

The Worst Thing You Can Do

The worst thing you can do is sit around and think about yourself. Some people do just that — they sit around and think about themselves and their problems. When all you do is sit around and think about yourself and your problems, it's like digging yourself deeper and deeper into a ditch. It makes it seem like things are getting worse and worse, whether they are or not, because all you're doing is thinking about your issues. *That isn't healthy for anyone*, whether you're a believer or not, but especially if you're a believer, you need to keep your mind off of yourself.

Do you know people who talk non-stop about themselves? People who say, "Well, me and my husband have this issue going on, and my kids are doing that, and this is happening with our finances, and we have that challenge...." When you talk to these kinds of people, it can be overwhelming. You wonder if they are ever going to take a break and breathe. It's like they never stop, and from beginning to end, they talk and talk about themselves and all their issues. Then at the very end of the conversation, when it's time for everybody to leave, almost in a clumsy way they say, "You know what? Time is up and I never even asked you how you are doing!" By that time, you're so exhausted you probably don't even want to tell them how you're doing. And you really don't think they want to know anyway because all they've done is focus on themselves. This is not healthy for anyone to do, and it's not healthy for you or the friends who have to listen to it either.

If this example describes you, you need to get your mind off of yourself and do something for someone else. But rest assured, you are not alone. This has always been a problem because thinking about yourself is part of human nature.

When we read Philippians 2:4, the Bible says, "Look not every man on his own things, but every man also on the things of others." A good habit we can all practice in our personal lives is that when we meet people, choose to immediately focus on them. Decide you want to know who they are, who their parents are, how they were raised, what they believe, what their business is, and what their dreams are. Try to focus on them because we are called to serve others.

It has always been the tendency of human beings to focus on themselves. That's why the apostle Paul wrote, "Look not every man on his own things...." This is a command. Verse 4 goes on to say, "...but every man [look] also on the things of others." This means that we need to get our minds off ourselves, and we need to start thinking of others.

In Philippians 2:19-21, Paul talks about Timothy and how precious Timothy was to him. This is what he said:

> **But I trust in the Lord Jesus to send Timotheus shortly unto you, that I also may be of good comfort, when I know your**

state. For I have no man likeminded, who will naturally care for your state. For all seek their own....
— Philippians 2:19-21

It is truly a gift when you find a person that is more focused on others than he is on himself, but this is the command of God. It is unhealthy for you if all you're doing is thinking about yourself and your own issues. For you to be spiritually healthy, you need to have the ingredient of doing something for someone else in your life and in your spiritual diet. And you need to try to do something for someone else at least once a day.

We Are Called To Serve One Another 'Without Grudging'

In his letters, Peter made some amazing statements about serving others and using the gifts that God has placed in our lives:

Use hospitality one to another without grudging.
— 1 Peter 4:9

This looks like a very small verse, but in fact, this verse is *jam-packed* with insight. For example, when Peter said "use hospitality," he used the Greek word *philoxenos*. The word *philos* is the Greek word for *a friend* or *to be friendly*, and the word *xenos* depicts *an alien* either living in or passing through a city or a foreign country, thus *a foreigner*. It could also be translated as *a guest*, *a stranger*, or *a traveler*. When you compound the two words together, they form the word *philoxenos*, which depicts *the attitude and actions of one who is helpful and hospitable to aliens in a foreign city or country, one who is helpful and hospitable to those who are out of their element, or one who is helpful and hospitable to strangers*. It can even mean *one who is helpful and hospitable to anyone in a struggling position*.

When Peter used this word in his letter, he was instructing believers to realize that having this kind of attitude toward one another is a command of Scripture. The Bible tells us that we need to get our minds off of ourselves and look around to see people who are out of their element or people who are going through difficult times. We are commanded to see what we can do to help them. In fact, we are told to befriend them.

It is a standing command of Scripture for all believers to have an openheart mentality to see what they can do for others. But if you're only thinking about yourself, you're not going to have this mentality. Notice

Peter said that we are to use hospitality "one to another." In the Greek, "one to another" is the word *allelous*, which means *one to another*, and it describes *a reciprocal behavior that is to be mutually exchanged between believers when a need arises.* This tells us we are to show hospitality reciprocally to each other.

Peter went on to say in verse 9 that we are to do this "without grudging." The word "without" is the Greek word *aneu* — a preposition that means *to do something in accompaniment, to do something in cooperation,* or *to do something parallel to another action.* In the context of verse 9, Peter used "without" to command all believers not to sing a bad duet, or not to help others with a resentful attitude. Helping someone with a resentful attitude is like saying, "I'm going to do it, but I don't want to do it." You should not serve others with the accompaniment of grumbling or grudging.

The word "grudging" in this verse literally means *to begrudge, complain, grumble, loath, moan, and groan,* or *to quietly mutter resentment under one's breath.* In context, it pictures one who accommodates those who are struggling, but rather than doing it joyfully, he does it with the accompaniment of silent resentment, inward complaining, grumbling, or muttering under his breath.

The following is the *Renner Interpretive Version* (*RIV*) of First Peter 4:9:

> **Be reciprocally helpful and hospitable especially to fellow believers who find themselves in a foreign or unfamiliar territory, who are out of their natural element, or who are in a struggling position, and do it without the accompaniment or begrudging, bellyaching, groaning, grumbling, moaning, or griping under your breath.**

Peter was stating that as believers we are called to serve one another without resentful attitudes. There is no way around it — this is a command that every believer should follow and, as we will see, it is also something God has uniquely gifted us to do.

God Has Given You Wonderful Gifts!

Peter went on to write in First Peter 4:10: "As every man hath received the gift, even so minister the same one to another, as good stewards of the manifold grace of God."

Notice at the very beginning of this verse, Peter said "every man." In the Greek, this is the word *hekastos*, and it means *every man, without exception*. According to this verse, *every man, without exception*, has received "the gift." The word "gift" is the Greek word *charisma*, which describes *a grace-given gift*. This is a gift that empowers you to do something you probably would not be able to do by yourself — it is *a supernaturally given gift*.

God has given every man, without exception, a supernatural, grace-given gift — and that includes you and me! Every single one of us has received this wonderful gift. And this gift is not intended to be only for us — *this gift is meant to be given to others*. We are to serve one another with these gifts. That's why in verse 10 Peter went on to say, "even so minister the same one to another, as good stewards of the manifold grace of God."

The word "minister" is the Greek word *diakoneo*, which was a word used to describe *a servant whose primary responsibility was to serve food and to wait on tables*. It presents a picture of *a waiter who painstakingly tends to the needs and wishes of a patron*. It was this servant's supreme task to please clients, and therefore, he served honorably, pleasurably, and in a fashion that made the people he waited on feel as if they were nobility. This word described *a committed, professional server — one who was zealously dedicated to doing his job at the highest level possible*.

By choosing this word, Peter alerts you and me to the fact that God expects us to be passionately committed to using the gifts He has given us in such a way that pleases Him and makes those whom we are serving feel as if they're kings and queens. That is God's will for us — *that we excellently serve with the gift that he has placed in us*. But if we're only thinking about ourselves, we are not going to be in a position to serve anyone else. It is time for us to get our mind off ourselves and begin to think about how we can use our gift to serve others.

You Are Called To Be a Good Steward

Notice that Peter also said we are to be good stewards of the "manifold grace of God" (1 Peter 4:10). The word "manifold" is the Greek word *poikilos*, which means *assorted, diverse, various, variegated*, or *multicolored*. A form of this word, "manifold," is also used in the Old Testament Greek Septuagint to describe Joseph's coat of many colors. Peter used it here to denote the assorted, diverse, various, variegated, multifaceted, and multicolored gifts of grace that God has entrusted to His people.

Here is the *Renner Interpretive Version* (*RIV*) of First Peter 4:10:

> **Accordingly, as every single one of you (with no exceptions) has received a grace-given charisma, you need to continuously minister to and serve one another with those gifts to the best of your ability and with the highest possible standard. God has assigned this great responsibility to you, so administrate and manage what He has entrusted to you as outstanding managers of the assorted, diverse, various, variegated, multifaceted, and multicolored manifestations of the grace of God.**

All of that is in you, and God wants your unique gifts and flavor to show up in your life. He wants His grace-given gifts to be released so they can begin to bless those around you. But again, if you're just sitting around thinking about yourself, *it's going to squash all those gifts in you.* This is why doing something for someone is such an essential element that you need in your spiritual diet. Get your mind off of yourself and begin to look for those around you who have needs and serve them without bellyaching or a begrudging attitude — *it will cause you to be set free from yourself.*

STUDY QUESTIONS

> Study to shew thyself approved unto God, a workman that needeth not to be ashamed, rightly dividing the word of truth
> — 2 Timothy 2:15

1. What is the command we are given in First Peter 4:9?
2. What is the translation of the Greek word *allelous*? What does this word mean for believers in the context of First Peter 4:9?
3. Which Greek word did Peter specifically use to alert believers that God expects us to be passionately committed to using the gifts He has given us in such a way that pleases Him and meets the needs of others?

PRACTICAL APPLICATION

> But be ye doers of the word, and not hearers only, deceiving your own selves
> — James 1:22

1. In this lesson, Rick mentions that one of the worst things you can do is sit around and just think about yourself — your needs and your problems. Take a moment to honestly ask yourself, *if someone played a recording back to you or simply told you what they hear you talk about all the time, how would you feel?*
2. Think about some ways you can practice thinking and putting the needs of others ahead of your own. List them here and make a conscious effort to put them into practice in your daily life.

LESSON 4

TOPIC

Say 'No' to Some Things

SCRIPTURES

1. **Titus 2:11,12 (*NIV*)** — For the grace of God has appeared that offers salvation to all people. It teaches us to say "No" to ungodliness and worldly passions, and to live self-controlled, upright and godly lives in this present age.
2. **Psalm 19:12,13** — Who can understand his errors? cleanse thou me from secret faults. Keep back thy servant also from presumptuous sins; let them not have dominion over me....

GREEK WORDS
No Greek words were shown on the TV program.

SYNOPSIS
It is important to take care of your physical health, and in order to do this, there are some essential things you need to have in your life. It is no different for your spiritual health. There are also essential ingredients that you need in your spiritual diet if you want to stay spiritually healthy and strong. But you need to know what these essential ingredients are before you can begin practicing them in your spiritual life. In previous lessons, you've learned that the ingredients you need to have a healthy spiritual diet are: *spending time with God every day*, *being quiet and praying*, and

doing something for someone else. In today's lesson, you will learn all about the next ingredient, which is *you need to say "no" to some things.* It may be obvious that you should not participate in sinful activities, but you should also say "no" to things that will cause you to stress or put you in strife. If your plate is too full, it will prevent you from doing the things that God has called you to do, and it may prevent others around you from growing and fulfilling the call on their life as well.

The emphasis of this lesson is:

There are certain things you should not eat in order to stay physically healthy. There are also some things you need to say "no" to in order to stay spiritually healthy. According to Titus 2:11 and 12, the grace of God teaches us to say "no" to ungodliness and worldly passions and, instead, to live self-controlled, upright, and godly lives. You will learn in this lesson that if you must touch everything, you will never grow very far because you can only reach so far. If you learn to let things go, your life will be more peaceful and more productive.

The Importance of Saying 'No'

In this lesson, you will learn about the next essential ingredient that you need in your spiritual diet. To review, in the first lesson you learned about the most important ingredient of all: you need to spend time with God, especially in the mornings. The second ingredient you need is to be quiet and pray. While it may seem challenging to find the time to be quiet, you learned that you can carve out time even for one or two minutes a day, and doing this allows the Lord to minister to your heart and show you things you may not have seen otherwise. In the last lesson, you learned about the third ingredient you need in your spiritual diet, which is that you need to do something for someone else. You saw that it is not healthy for anyone to sit and wallow in their own problems and that when you get your mind off yourself and begin to think of how you can help others, your mind will feel less clouded and your God-given gifts will become more and more developed.

But in this lesson, you will learn about ingredient number four, which is *you need to say "no" to some things.* This is an essential part of your spiritual diet. Just like there are certain things you shouldn't eat in order to remain physically healthy, there are also things you should say "no" to in order to stay spiritually strong. For example, if all you eat is ice cream and key lime pie, your body is going to end up in trouble. It's okay to have dessert from time to time, but you also have to practice self-control and say "no" to dessert sometimes too. If you say "yes" to everything that's put on your plate, you're going to be in trouble — *and it's the same way in your spiritual life.*

The *New International Version* of Titus 2:11 and 12 reads, "For the grace of God has appeared that offers salvation to all people. It teaches us to say 'No' to ungodliness and worldly passions, and to live self-controlled, upright and godly lives in this present age." So the grace of God teaches us to say "no" to some things. *What does it teach us to say "no" to?* It teaches us to say "no" to ungodliness and to worldly passions. But notice it says that we're to live self-controlled lives. If you are just saying "yes" to everything that is presented to you, you are not exercising self-control. There are things you are supposed to say "no" to simply because *you're not supposed to do them.*

The Danger of Presumptuous Sin

David made an amazing statement about this in Psalm 19:12 and 13. He said:

> **Who can understand his errors? cleanse thou me from secret faults. Keep back thy servant also from presumptuous sins; let them not have dominion over me....**

In this passage, David asked God to protect him from "presumptuous sins." What is presumptuous sin? Essentially, it is the sin of assuming you are to do something without praying and asking God about it first. If you commit this kind of sin and do not repent of it, it will end up having dominion over your life.

Maybe you are someone who feels like you don't have the ability to say "no" very easily. Perhaps even when you do say "no" you feel guilty, so you're driven to say "yes" to every single thing that you're asked to do. If this sounds like you and you feel like life has gotten out of control, your presumptuous commitments have likely taken dominion over your life.

This is something that Rick has struggled with in the past. For years he assumed that he was supposed to say "yes" to every need that was presented to him. This was especially true when he first moved to the territory of the former Soviet Union. When he moved to this part of the world, it was quite frankly in a mess. It was bankrupt and broken — there was no money, there was a deficit of goods, and people saw Rick as the stereotypical American who had a lot of money. Whether it was true or not, they assumed it to be true. Rick knew that even though he didn't have a lot of money, he probably had more than others had, so when people came to him and asked for help or assistance, he couldn't bear to say "no." He would say "yes" to nearly everyone. This was also a moment when God was telling Rick to say "yes" to a lot things to grow the ministry; however, he couldn't do what God was telling him to do because he had said "yes" to so many things that God had not told him to do.

In his eagerness to help, Rick had made commitments to pay for various things, and at the end of the day, he didn't have enough money to pay the bills of his own ministry because he had wrongly assumed he was to pay for every need that was presented to him. All of those presumptuous sins literally took dominion over him, and Rick had to make a real adjustment to the way he thought — *he had to learn to say "no."*

Say 'No' to Things You Don't Need To Do

Learning to say "no" is one of the most difficult lessons you'll ever learn, but it is essential for you to be spiritually strong. And not only that, in the earlier days of Rick's ministry, another presumptuous sin he had was assuming that he had to be a part of everything. He was in every meeting and a part of every decision that was made. If he ended up not attending a meeting, Rick felt guilty that he wasn't there. He wondered, *What will people think if I'm not at work or not in a meeting?* He was driven by guilt of what people would think, and therefore, he ended up attending meetings that he didn't need to be in and making decisions that other people could have decided. All of these presumptuous ways of thinking dominated his life and eventually nearly deteriorated his health. Rick had to learn to say "no" to the things he didn't need to be doing as well as release other people to do what they were better at doing than he was. By saying "yes" to everything and trying to have a hand in every decision, *Rick was robbing people of opportunities that God had called them to do.*

When you say "yes" to everything, you really do rob others of opportunities to do what God has called them to do. This is a hard lesson to learn, but it's one that will set you free. Rick had to learn to let go, and in turn, he learned a very important lesson — *if you have to put your hands on everything, then whatever you're growing is not going to grow very far because your arms can only reach so far.* If you have to touch everything, then what you're working on is only going to grow as far as you can reach. But God has likely brought other people with capable hands to work alongside you, and you can touch them and they can touch others and so on. You need to let other people do what they are called to do. Ask yourself, *Who has God called to help me so that I don't have to do everything?*

This applies to finances as well. Don't feel obligated to say "yes" to every need that is presented to you. Of course, if the Lord speaks to you and tells you to say "yes," then you need to be obedient and do what He says. But before you say "yes" to every project that is presented to you, you should pray first. Say, "Lord, is this a task for me, or is this an assignment that you have for someone else?" You don't want to take somebody else's blessing. Do what God tells you to say "yes" to, but don't commit to what God tells you to say "no" to — *be God-led in whom you help.*

Say 'No' to Things Someone Else Can Do

One important principle that Rick shares in the program is this: 85 percent of what you do someone else can do; ten percent of what you do someone else can be trained to do; and five percent of what you do only you can do. This means that the five percent only you can do is the most important part of what you do. Although, in reality most people can't do their five percent because they've committed to do the 85 percent of work that somebody else could be doing or the ten percent of what they do that somebody else could be trained to do. And because they are giving themselves to 95 percent of things that other people should be doing, they can't get around to the five percent that only they can do. These people should say "yes" to fewer things and, instead, say "no" to more things.

Rick has learned over the years that you need to back off of saying "yes" to that ninety-five percent other people can do and really focus on your five percent. Your five percent is important — *really important.* It's the five percent that nobody else can do but you. And if you don't do your five percent, it's going to negatively affect those around you. But if you do your five percent and do it well, it is going to *empower* those around you. Don't say "yes" to things that you should be saying "no" to. Before you make a decision, take a step back and say, "Okay, I understand that this needs to be done, but is this something that somebody else should do? Or does this fit into my five percent?" If it's something someone else should do, let that person know and allow them to fulfill what God has called them to do too.

Part of Rick's five percent is his work in the ministry. For example, he sits in his chair and teaches, and right now there is no one else who can sit in his chair and do what he does. He exegetes from the Greek New Testament, and although he has editors and people who help him in many ways, he is still the only one in the ministry that exegetes from the Greek New Testament. Rick is also the only one in the ministry who has the ears to hear the direction from the Lord for the ministry. This is part of his five percent — the five percent that he is supposed to shine in. But if he is doing the 85 percent that somebody else could do, or the ten percent that somebody could be trained to do, and never get around to his five percent, it would affect the entire ministry. The ministry would never grow as God intended it to grow.

It messes up everything when you over-commit and say "yes" to what you're supposed to be saying "no" to. It may sound basic but learning to say "no" to the things someone else can do will liberate you — *it will totally set you free*. You must learn how to do your part, the part that nobody else can do for you. And remember, when you focus on your part, it liberates others to do their parts too. Everybody flourishes because everybody is where they're supposed to be, doing what they're supposed to be doing.

Say 'No' to Your Own Ideas

You must also learn to say "no" to some of your own ideas. For instance, Rick wakes up every day with new ideas. He's an idea guy — he is a fountain of ideas — but he has had to come to grips with the fact that not all of his ideas are God-sent ideas. Some of them are just Rick's ideas, and sometimes he has to say "no" to them. He has to discern which ones are from the Lord and which ones are his own. One thing that helps Rick do this is bringing his ideas to the men that God has put in his life to help oversee him. They talk to him about his ideas, his assignments, and the projects he wants to begin. They help him discern whether these are really God-given or whether they are just his own.

It is very important that you have people in your life who help keep you in balance. Don't get into the business of presumptuous sins and presuming that you're to do everything because in the end you'll lose control of *everything*. Find wise, godly people who can help you identify these areas of over-commitment and who can keep you accountable to what God has called you to do.

So to review, you've learned that every day you need to spend time with God, you need to be quiet and pray, and you need to do something for someone else. In this lesson, you've also seen that there are just some things you need to say "no" to. In the next lesson, you will discover the fifth essential ingredient you need in order to maintain a healthy spiritual diet — *you need to stir up the gift of God that is inside of you.*

STUDY QUESTIONS

Study to shew thyself approved unto God, a workman that needeth not to be ashamed, rightly dividing the word of truth.
— 2 Timothy 2:15

1. Why is it important to say "no" to some things? What does saying "yes" too often prohibit you from doing?
2. According to Psalm 19:12 and 13, what are "presumptuous sins"?
3. Who has God placed in your life to help you get things done? How can you rely on these people more and do less yourself?

PRACTICAL APPLICATION

But be ye doers of the word, and not hearers only, deceiving your own selves.
— James 1:22

1. In this lesson, Rick shared the principle that 85 percent of what you do could be done by someone else, ten percent of what you do someone could be trained to do, and five percent of what you do can only be done by you. Take a moment to break down what you do into these three categories and then reflect on your answers. Really think about what you could be saying "no" to and in what areas you may be overcommitting.
2. Rick mentions having a close group of people that help oversee him and help him sort through which ideas are God-ideas and which are not. Think about the people you have in your life who you could talk to about the things you should be saying "yes" and "no" to. Write their names down and make an effort to go to these people in times when you feel you may be tempted to overcommit yourself.

LESSON 5

TOPIC
Stir Up the Gift of God Inside You

SCRIPTURES
1. **1 John 3:9** — Whosoever is born of God doth not commit sin; for his seed remaineth in him: and he cannot sin, because he is born of God.
2. **2 Timothy 1:6** — Wherefore I put thee in remembrance that thou stir up the gift of God, which is in thee by the putting on of my hands

GREEK WORDS
1. "seed" — **σπέρμα** (*sperma*): seed; seed of all kinds — animal, human, and vegetation; sperm
2. "stir up" — **ἀναζωπυρέω** (*anadzoopureo*): the Greek words **ἀνά** (*ana*), **ζῶον** (*zoon*), and **πῦρ** (*pur*); the word **ἀνά** (*ana*) carries the idea of repeating an earlier action or doing something again; the word **ζῶον** (*zoon*) is from a root that means to be enthusiastic, to be fervent, to be passionate, to be vigorous, to be wholehearted, or to be zealous; the word **πῦρ** (*pur*) is the Greek word for fire; it must be noted that in Classical Greek, fire was a life-giving force and it was used on the hearths of every ancient home to keep people warm; it was also used in matters related to the divine and supernatural and it was used as a force to defeat enemies; fire was so central to life that human life was unsustainable without it

SYNOPSIS
In this lesson, we will wrap up our teaching about what you need in your spiritual diet. The final ingredient is that *you need to stir up the gift of God inside you.* Just like you need to use a fork to lift food from a plate to your mouth, you must also stir up the gifts of God inside you in order for them to operate. The moment you were born again, the seed of God was placed inside you, and that seed contains everything that God is. But you must use that seed in order for it to grow and for your spiritual fire to burn bright. Anybody's fire can start to dim when the gifts within them are not being stirred. Even Timothy needed to be reminded by Paul to stir up the

gift of God in him (*see* 2 Timothy 1:6). We will see in this lesson that we all have a responsibility to *stir up the gift of God* that is within us.

The emphasis of this lesson is:

For our final lesson, you will learn that you need to *stir up the gift of God that is inside you*. This means that to stir up your gifts, you need to be proactive. You can't eat without actually picking up food and putting it in your mouth, and it's the same with your spiritual gifts. Just seeing food on your plate does not mean it's going to end up in your mouth — you've got to do something to get it into your mouth. Likewise, just because there's a gift in you that does not mean it's going to automatically operate in your life — *you have to stir it up*.

In our very first lesson, we discussed the importance of spending time with God, especially in the mornings. In our second lesson, we looked at why we need to be quiet and pray every day. Our third lesson explained the necessity of doing something for someone else. In the last lesson, we also learned why it is important to say "no" to some things. In this lesson, we'll learn why we need to *stir up the gift of God that is inside us*.

What Is the Gift of God Inside You?

First John 3:9 says, "Whosoever is born of God doth not commit sin; for his seed remaineth in him: and he cannot sin, because he is born of God." The word "seed" in Greek is the word *sperma*, which is where we get the word "sperm." This word "seed" describes seeds of all kinds — animal seed, human seed, and vegetation seed — but in Greek, it is the word *sperma*. A literal translation would be that God's sperm is in you, which means the day you said yes to Jesus and the Holy Spirit came into you, the divine seed of God came into you as well. And in that seed is the life of God, the DNA of God, the power of God, and the character of God — *everything that God is came inside you the moment you were saved*.

This is truly amazing! But in order for the seed of God to become activated in your life, you need to stir up what is inside you. In Second Timothy 1:6, the apostle Paul wrote to Timothy about doing just that. Timothy was in a very difficult position, and he was probably thinking about how to protect himself — how to protect himself from assault and how to insulate himself from the pressures around him — but this is never a very good way to think. Paul told Timothy that he needed to get his mind off of himself and that he needed to stir up the gift of God inside him. Paul wrote:

> **Wherefore I put thee in remembrance that thou stir up the gift of God, which is in thee by the putting on of my hands.**
> **— 2 Timothy 1:6**

This is the case for all of us. God already did His part when He put His seed in you, but now it's up to you to stir it up.

'Stir Up' the Gift God Has Given You

You might be wondering, *What does it mean to stir up the gift of God in you?* "Stir up" is the Greek word *anadzoopureo*, which is a compound of three Greek words. First, there's the word *ana*, which carries the idea of *repeating an action or doing something again*. The second word is the word *zoon*, which is from a root which means *to be enthusiastic, to be fervent, to be passionate, to be vigorous, to be wholehearted*, or *to be zealous*. The third word in this compound is the word *pur*, which is the word for *fire*. It is important to note that in the ancient world fire was a life-giving force that was used on the hearths of every ancient home to keep people warm. It was used in matters that related to the divine and the supernatural, and it was used as a force to defeat enemies. Fire was so central to life that human life was unsustainable without it. But when you compound each of these three words together — *ana*, *zoon*, and *pur* — it is translated *stir up*.

The use of this word in Second Timothy 1:6 tells us that Timothy's fire was on a low burn. By using the word *ana*, Paul was saying, "Hey, Timothy, you need to go back to the beginning and do what you once did. You need to do it again." He told Timothy that he needed to stir up the gift of God that was inside of him already — *wow!*

The word *anadzoopureo* pictures a person who goes to his furnace, or to his fireplace, and he sees that the fireplace is on a low ebb — the embers are beginning to go out, and rather than just look at it and say, "Oh, it's so sad that my coals are going out," he becomes proactive. He picks up his poker and gets new fuel for the fire. He takes his poker and begins to stir those coals until finally, once again, there is a raging fire in the fireplace.

A Real-Life Example of Stirring Your Spiritual Flame

This was all theory to Rick until his family moved to the former Soviet Union. When the Renners moved to the former Soviet Union, there was no such thing as central heating. In fact, *to this day* they have no such thing in Russia as central air, but especially back in those days, in the houses Rick's family lived in, they had coal heat. They had to learn how to stoke the coals to keep the fire burning, and they learned that they had to work on those coals all day long. They couldn't assume that they were going to have heat all day just because they had it in the morning. Even when they worked the coals in the morning, it didn't take long for those coals to begin to go out. Likewise, if you want to keep your spiritual fire burning, you must keep putting more fuel into the fire and you must work and work those coals. In fact, to really keep the fire burning within you, you need to pay attention to those coals about once every hour.

When Rick and Denise moved to the city of Riga with their sons, they moved into a house that was supposed to have central, city-wide heating by the winter. And by city-wide heating, they meant radiator heating, not central air. Even though the city installed all new pipes and got everything ready for the central heating system, they never turned it on in Rick and Denise's building. That part of the world can get pretty cold during the winter, and when winter came, their family was walking around the house in big coats and could even see their breath inside their house. But the Renners' house, which was an apartment in the middle of Riga, Latvia, did have fireplaces. Not fireplaces like you would probably imagine — these were big furnaces that were over a hundred years old! While these fireplaces were beautifully decorated, they were useless because the Renners had no fuel.

It doesn't do any good to have a fireplace or furnace if you don't have any fuel. And because Rick and Denise's family lived in the center of the city, they couldn't transport any fuel to their home. So there they were, living with their family in a big apartment that was so cold they could see their own breath.

One day Rick and Denise were sitting in the living room in their coats — Denise had on a hat and gloves too — and suddenly, their sons threw on their coats and ran out the front door. Rick said to Denise, "I wonder where they're going?" Soon the boys came back through the door carrying armloads of wood. Rick then said to the boys, "Where did you get that wood?" And here's where they got it: the Renners' apartment was the first apartment to be renovated in their entire building. That means that all the other apartments were derelict and had completely fallen to ruin. The apartment below them was *so ruined and so derelict that it didn't have any windows.* This contributed to their cold situation because the wind and cold air was blowing freely through that entire apartment which affected the temperature in their apartment. The boys had gone down to that apartment and pulled up pieces of the parquet floors. Those floors were so ruined that the parquet was warped and some of it was even burned. The boys had said to each other, "Hey, we know where to get some fuel!" and then went down to that apartment and began to rip up the parquet. It was amazing parquet, but it could not have been restored because it was so ruined. So the boys ripped up that flooring, came walking back into their apartment with armloads of old parquet, and began to put it into the central furnace in the apartment. They lit a fire, and soon the furnace was putting out heat. The Renners *finally* had heat in the furnace, but to keep the heat burning, they had to keep putting more fuel into the fire.

The Renners had a very long metal poker, and every member of their family learned how to open the door to the furnace, put the poker into the furnace, and stir those embers to keep the fire burning. The fire was not going to continually burn by itself — it required their participation. And if they had chosen to ignore those embers, then they would have had to reap the consequences of being cold.

Don't Let Your Spiritual Coals Grow Cold

Maybe this has happened to you. Maybe there was a time when the fire of God was raging in your life but because you got busy and other things got your attention, time has gone by and you've fallen out of the habit of stirring the coals — *you're no longer burning like you once spiritually burned.* So what do you do? Here's what you do: you don't sit around and say, "I wish I was like I used to be," or, "I wish that somebody would come lay their hands on me." Paul didn't say that to Timothy. Paul told him, "Timothy, it's up to you — it's your furnace, it's your heart, and what takes place in your heart is up to you." So just like Timothy, when the fire of God within you is burning low, *you need to be spiritually proactive.*

To stir the fire in you, you need to add more fuel to the fire, stick your poker into the fire, stoke the coals, and fan the flames. Do this over and over again just like you used to do it. *This is an essential part of your spiritual diet.* Part of it involves reading the Bible, part of it involves praying in tongues, part of it involves serving others, part of it involves using your gifts, and part of it involves using your faith. Each of these things are part of the poker that stirs the flame deep inside your heart. If you want the gift of God in your life to really burn, *you are responsible to stir it up*. God did His part by putting His seed in you — God did the greatest thing — but now it's up to you to fan it into a great, raging flame of fire. If you humbly ask the Holy Spirit and seek Him out, He will show you how to *stir up the gift of God inside you*.

STUDY QUESTIONS

Study to shew thyself approved unto God, a workman that needeth not to be ashamed, rightly dividing the word of truth.
— 2 Timothy 2:15

1. What is the Greek translation of First John 3:9? What does it mean to have God's seed planted in you?
2. The Greek word for "stir up" is *anadzoopureo*. You learned that *anadzoopureo* is a compound of three words. List them and their meanings below. What does their compounded meaning depict, and how does it correlate to stirring up the gift of God inside you?
3. What things can you do to stoke your spiritual embers and stir up your spiritual flame?

PRACTICAL APPLICATION

But be ye doers of the word, and not hearers only, deceiving your own selves.
— James 1:22

1. Use what you learned in this lesson to list some ways in which you can actively stir up the gift of God in your life.
2. Honestly ask yourself what your spiritual flame looks like. Is it a raging fire, or is it beginning to wane? Write down some ways in which you can tend to your inner flame — like a poker stoking hot coals in a furnace.

Notes

Notes

CLAIM YOUR FREE RESOURCE!

As a way of introducing you further to the teaching ministry of Rick Renner, we would like to send you FREE of charge his teaching, "How To Receive a Miraculous Touch From God" on CD or USB format.

In His earthly ministry, Jesus commonly healed *all* who were sick of *all* their diseases. In this profound message, learn about the manifold dimensions of Christ's wisdom, goodness, power, and love toward all humanity who came to Him in faith with their needs.

☑ YES, I want to receive Rick Renner's monthly teaching letter!

Simply scan the QR code to claim this resource or go to:
renner.org/claim-your-free-offer

WITH US!

R renner.org

- facebook.com/rickrenner • facebook.com/rennerdenise
- youtube.com/rennerministries • youtube.com/deniserenner
- instagram.com/rickrenner • instagram.com/rennerministries_
  instagram.com/rennerdenise

Printed in the USA
CPSIA information can be obtained
at www.ICGtesting.com
LVHW020439260823
756142LV00014BA/341